About the Author

Rindala Awad was born in 1978 in Beirut during the civil war, where she grew up, before emigrating from Lebanon to Canada at the age of nine. She obtained her masters in architecture from McGill University in Montreal, then began a career that carried her out from the destruction she lived through in Lebanon towards the imagination and the creation of incredible forms and buildings. Through this novel, she shares with us a sensible story of her path and her origins.

My Dearest Mother

Rindala

My Dearest Mother

Olympia Publishers
London

www.olympiapublishers.com
OLYMPIA PAPERBACK EDITION

A CIP catalogue record for this title is
available from the British Library.

ISBN: 978-1-80439-048-1

This book is memoir. It reflects the author's present recollections of
experiences over time. Some names and characteristics have been
changed, some events have been compressed, and some dialogue
has been recreated.

First Published in 2023

Olympia Publishers
Tallis House
2 Tallis Street
London
EC4Y 0AB

Printed in Great Britain

Dedication

To my father

Acknowledgement

I would like to extend my sincere gratitude to Nadia Hemady, for her sensible and eloquent translation of this book from French to English.

My dearest mother,

If you only knew everything that has happened, I do not know how you would feel, but in a few words, I would like to tell you.

"I don't know if it was a dream or something that really happened."

"That doesn't matter, go on, keep telling me," replied Corine.

I began.

She was seated in bed, her eyes swollen, unable to see very well. Her smile conveyed her suffering in a soft and gentle way. The nurse entered the room and placed a plate of food on her bed. I approached the plate to take a bite of cheese when I heard my mother, who was standing next to my father and brother, say to me, "That's for your mother!"

My mother? But who is my mother? Isn't it you? I asked myself.

At that moment, I experienced a paralysing feeling of anguish mixed with confusion. I did not know whether I should take the piece of cheese or leave it, and in seeing this woman disappear forever from my life, a deep sense of guilt settled inside of me. This feeling of guilt persists within me because each time I make a decision, I feel that I am holding on to a part and relinquishing another part, that may disappear forever.

Chapter 1

Essence of Life and a Betrayed Childhood

That apartment on the third floor of a seven-storey building in which we lived faced the main street, Hamra. Surrounded by windows, it had two large balconies; one facing the back alley and the other the main road.

With the sun shining through the shades, I opened my eyes to the sound of my grandmother's voice. I found her sitting at a little table in the kitchen with a friend, a cup of coffee, some biscuits, butter and marmalade. She spent some time talking about her life and her family in Bolivia and Chile.

Abuelita, my grandmother, who was born in Chile, left her home country at the age of ten to go live in Bolivia, and then again at the age of forty-three to come live in Lebanon. With her, we spoke Spanish, and over the years I came to understand that my grandmother and my father were Lebanese 'ex-pats' in their own country.

The room that my brothers and I shared was connected to the kitchen from the other side of the house by long, spacious hallways. Those hallways of marble that went from our room all the way to the kitchen passed first through a foyer, followed by the family room to the left, the living room to the right and the main entrance down the hall. The hallway then changed direction, continuing past the dining room and ending up at the kitchen.

The family room was connected to the dining room, on the other side of which one reached a balcony that looked out over the backyard. The family room, with its brown sofas and television set, was at the centre of our home, a warm hearth where we spent the evenings watching television and eating toast Abuelita prepared for us. My grandfather, Abuelito, enjoyed listening to the singing of improvised poetry known as *daloonah*. With all of us seated around him, we passed the evenings listening to those traditional songs, always preceded by the national anthem of Lebanon that the television channel broadcast every night.

That hallway that always seemed so vast and infinite served for us as a world of games and fantasy; a highway where my brother drove his little metallic cars, a marble rink for us to skate across, a labyrinth at night by candlelight for our games of hide and seek, and all of the other games that our imaginations could conceive.

In the rectangular foyer in front of our bedroom, there was a door that led to my grandparents' room, another door opposite that one which belonged to my father and stepmother, and a third door leading to the bathroom. The foyer was large enough to hold a desk where my brother did his homework. And right next to the hallway, there was an ancient sewing machine with a foot pedal. By the light of a candle and the sound of the pedal that operated the machine, I stood beside Abuelita, bent over with her glasses on, so I could watch her sew and feel her presence in the darkness. Her closeness was a silent balm for all my worries.

That darkness which descended on our apartment set the perfect stage for our games of hide-and-go-seek in the house with my grandfather. My favourite hiding spot was behind the refrigerator in the kitchen where we waited, our hearts racing, for my brother to find us. One time, when we heard my brother approaching, my grandfather picked me up quickly and placed me on top of the refrigerator, a wonderful hiding spot if I had only been able to hold in my laughter.

Abuelito took us on Sundays to play at the American University of Beirut, where we found a vast grassy field in the middle of the city. Surrounding the large field, there was a small forest where we played. One time, my grandfather instructed me to gather twigs. By placing the twigs one on top of the other, he built a tiny house for the birds.

Abuelito had a desk in a small room that was located at the end of the living room. He spent several hours each day there reading newspapers. These newspapers were piled right up to the ceiling; he kept them because he planned to write a book one day about the day-to-day political developments in Lebanon.

"Come!" He gestured for me to come and sit next to him.

I was perhaps three or four years old. I sat down next to him. He took out a paper and a crayon.

"Do you know how to draw a human figure?" he asked me.

I shook my head to tell him no. Slowly, he began to trace lines on the white sheet to make a small gentleman appear. It was so simple, yet somehow magical to watch this form appear on the white sheet. With his patience and simplicity, he entered my world.

In our room, next to my brother's bed, there was an armoire, but I was only able to see the outfits it contained once or twice. One day, I asked Abuelita what was inside that armoire and she replied, without looking at me, "Those are your mother's clothes."

It was the second time I had heard someone speak of this 'mother'. This is how I became, over the years, incredibly fascinated by this lady. I did not know how to get to know her because each revelation about her was followed by a silence.

Our apartment still held intimations of another reality, of something that had ceased to exist, but that one could neither hide nor forget, because it remained inscribed in traces, here and there. Over the years, I learned that there is no need to search in order to understand everything in a single instant, because the truth will eventually be unveiled.

Facing the family room, on the other side of the hallway, was the living room. This room was reserved for guests, with green floor-to-ceiling curtains and hand-stitched sofas sculpted from wood. On one side, there was large, slim-wheeled cart that held bottles and delicate glasses. And on a table at the end of the room, there was a statue, the bust of a woman with her neck extended, a pensive look on her face, hair pulled back in a ponytail. From the deep, protracted gaze of that woman, the sculpture emitted a sense of hope.

I entered frequently into that room in order to look at that statue that could not speak and which we never spoke about. At times, it seemed to me that we averted our gaze from her. She quickly became a subject to avoid, to keep silent about, but for me, I was consumed with curiosity to know who she was and why she was there.

The awareness that we have at a young age marks us and becomes a filter through which we view the world and by which we paint our own world.

The doorbell rang and I ran to the door after Abuelita to see who was there. Someone handed my grandmother gifts that had come from the United States. These gifts were not inexpensive.

"Why did we get presents?" I asked Abuelita.

Someone had thought of delighting us with these gifts and all of the other toys that filled the three or four shelves that ran along the wall of our room, as well as the toys packed away in the storage room. We had so many toys sent from friends and family far away.

The excessiveness of these gestures was in part an attempt to fill the void and ease the sadness that I had yet to understand. At times, it is the recognition of that which never was that ends up hurting us.

In spite of all these toys, we spent most of our time cultivating our imaginations through our apartment, in the hallways, behind the doors and curtains, and also on the two balconies, especially the one that faced the main road.

The balcony that faced the main road offered up a world of madness. With bed sheets hanging from the windows of our room and the balustrade of the balcony, we created the roof of our imaginary fort. With the sheets cloaking the length of the balustrade, we became invisible to the strangers on the first floor of the building.

We spent hours playing under the illusion that no one could find us. From time to time, I pulled the part draped over the balustrade away by a few centimetres to spy with one eye, my face pressed against the iron bars, the fat man on the balcony of the third or fourth floor of the building facing ours. This man sat for hours without moving so much as a muscle. My brother and I kept trying to get his attention, but we never succeeded. We came up with the idea of throwing toys at him to try and make him look at us, but our efforts drew no reaction from him. This went on until the day Abuelita saw us and scolded us severely, telling us that we should stop and ignore him. He then became a statue that existed as part of the scenery around us. A few times, I asked Abuelita who the man was but from her ambiguous responses, I figured out that it was better not to insist on knowing.

In the afternoons, once Abuelita had finished cleaning the kitchen after lunch, she left for several hours to have a coffee with our neighbours in the building. Silently, I sat next to her in order to listen to these women talk, a little of everything: the power outages and water cut-offs that interfered with their household routines, the daily challenge of walking up the stairs – when the elevators ceased to work – and all of the other troubles that had not previously existed. Their complaints were followed by pensive, distant looks, a silence and finally, my grandmother saying in Arabic, "What's the difference between you and me? We're all alike."

I heard those words among their sighs of exasperation mixed with the hope that perhaps one day the realisation that there really weren't any differences would become clear to the world's eyes and all troubles would disappear. That life would retrieve its rhythms and all that was happening now would pass.

During holidays, these ladies reunited in the evening by the light of candles, standing around our small kitchen table and making maamoul. With the scent of coffee from the coffee pot making the rounds of their cups, talking and laughing, they rolled the dough in their hands. They sculpted troughs, filled them with nuts and closed them again. With little metal pincers, they made incisions in the dough, partly as decoration and partly to create a ridged surface to hold the powder sugar we would sprinkle on top before eating them. With the trays filled up, Abuelita put them in the oven and took them out again once they were baked, followed by another plate, and then another plate, and so on, until the evening finished. From a short distance, I watched them.

I accompanied Abuelita everywhere, including her errands. We found her favourite vendors of fruits and vegetables. These vendors, their large carts piled up with produce, set up their stalls everywhere to sell the fruits of their harvest. At the end of our circuit, we stopped in a pastry shop and Abuelita treated me to a chocolate sable – my favourite type of pastry.

Mother, the Saturday mornings, when I accompanied Abuelita to the bakery to cook manaish, are among my most cherished memories. I woke up at five in the morning and we slipped out of the house while everyone was sleeping. It was calm, with only the crowing of the roosters and the sound of prayers from the mosques. We walked hand in hand to the bakery in the gentle light of dawn. At the entrance, we were welcomed by the smell of zaatar and hot bread and the flames of the oven further inside the restaurant. We waited for a place at the table. Standing, women and men prepared their manaish. They rolled the dough in a circle, spread zaatar and oil on top, and passed them to the end of the tables where the baker cooked them in the flames.

With Abuelita, my life was filled to brimming, especially with the energy she radiated; she overflowed with joy, smiles and friendship, in spite of it all.

Chapter 2

My Village

We spent several weeks in the village of my family in the north of Lebanon during our summer vacation. The car ride was the start of our adventure, which, after a journey of several hours, took us to the summit of the hills. We found ourselves looking down over clouds and deep valleys, in the midst of a carpet of trees and dark orange roofs. On the way, we travelled over several mountains that took us up above the clouds, far away from the reality that existed in Beirut.

In Hasroun, the village of my ancestors, we planned to stay for a few weeks at the house of Abuelito's sisters.

Leaving the car, I crossed a little road situated on a mountain top. Young boys and girls stood on the other side of the road, behind a fence, and watched me. I saw water gush from a hole in the mountain's rocky facade.

"Go on, drink, it's fresh water."

I approached to drink the flowing water; it was so cold and clear!

A few feet behind me, a man pushed a cart while calling out, "*Kaak... kaak.*"

Abuelita purchased a warm round of bread, sprinkled with grains (sesame seeds), and, along with the bread, a folded piece of white paper in which there was a dark red powder with a pleasantly sour taste.

"You can dip the *kaak* in the sumac," shouted one of the young girls from the other side of the road.

The girl came towards me and asked me to enter through the wooden fence and go down the path towards her house. I was curious to know what existed in the field, but before entering, I looked to Abuelita for permission.

"Don't stay too long, we just arrived and we should greet your aunts," Abuelita told me.

I was entranced to find myself on a green path, surrounded by white and black sheep. I approached them calmly, reaching out to touch a sheep for the first time. It was so soft!

Abuelita came to find me; it was time to go home. We crossed the little road on the edge of that hill to go to the garden of Tia Dolores. The garden led to the house which was located above, at the top of several stairways. On our way to the main house, which was a short distance away, we passed first by a smaller building that housed the kitchen. The house was built of cement, with a grey exterior that had long windows and green shades. It was a house both simple and majestic. The enormous living room area, comprising of four rooms, was located at the centre, with two additional rooms on each side of it.

One morning, my brother and I awoke, sick with fever. Abuelita told us to stay in bed so that we could rest, even though my brother and I wanted so much to go outside to play in the garden on that sunny morning.

My brother said to me, "I have an idea."

"What is it?" I replied.

"Before Abuelita comes to see us, let's press our

foreheads against the walls."

I understood immediately: the cement walls retained the night's coolness. We pressed our foreheads against the wall and waited for Abuelita to come in.

When we heard her approaching the door, we lay down properly in our beds again. She came towards me, touched my forehead and said, "Go on, you're fine. Go on and play."

There were stairs that ran down the length of the outer wall that led to the roof of the kitchen. We did not have permission to climb them because we could easily fall. That morning, I was overcome with curiosity to know what was up there, so I ascended the stairs quietly to see what I could see. Against the clear blue sky, the sun's rays and a gentle breeze streamed down through white drapes attached to a line. All around, there were plants that Tia Dolores had planted. I turned back, my heart pounding, as I saw Tia Dolores on her way up, because I knew that I was not supposed to be there. Her face scrunched up when she saw me, then after a few seconds, she beckoned me over. I sat down next to her without speaking. She took a tomato from one of the plants into her hand and squeezed it so that some of the juice dripped onto a piece of bread. She rolled up the bread and gave it to me. Even now, the taste of that tomato is vivid in my memory: through simple things we taste the truth.

By going along the unpaved streets of my village, we arrived in your village, Bcharré. The houses were built one next to the other. I looked out the window, seeking a pause in the rhythm of buildings that was interrupted by a stone arch, through which we found your childhood home.

The smell of coffee from the kitchen greeted us. At the end of the living room, a large patio opened up over the deepest valley. There was something incredible, yet intimate about the countryside.

I was walking towards the patio when I found you – large print photos, some of them on a table and others hanging on the wall.

"That's your mother," said Teita Ramza.

At dawn, Teita Ramza sat on the patio with a little cup of coffee. In the quiet serenity, she drank her coffee each morning while looking out over the valley. She did not speak much, but in her eyes lived the depths of times past. I truly loved finding her early in the morning for the *sobhie* as she called her early morning coffee. I sat with her, drinking coffee, which I adored even at eight years of age, and listened to the sound of the water flowing in the fountain.

There were two rooms next to the salon. My grandmother slept in one and my brother and I in the other. Opening my eyes, I watched the play of light on a table, which held a chariot of small perfume bottles that reflected the rays of light.

"She really loved perfumes," my Teita Ramza told me as she stood behind me. I was seated on the ground, staring at the perfumes, marvelling at the shifting colours.

In the afternoons, we went to play in the courtyard of the church where we found the other children of the village. My brother rushed off to play soccer with his friends from the village while I watched from a distance, the stone church looming over like a fortress at the end of the courtyard.

When we returned home in the evening, before the sun set, Teita Ramza would prepare toast for us with za'atar or labné.

Although much about our life was concealed, to distance and hide what was going on both within and without, the childhood that my brothers and I shared in our apartment and the mountain-top house above the valley, was both lovely and true. Sadness had no place in our world because we knew no other way of life. From my birth until I was nine years old, it was a world of discoveries, growth and realisations.

In the years following my childhood, I relived many of those memories in my mind, nostalgically, with sadness because I could not go back to those places, those moments, powerless and bound to the present. But I relived them with a big smile, remembering how much we enjoyed ourselves. We had no understanding of what was happening around us. It was all a game. The fear and danger were no more than an illusion. By Abuelita's side, nothing could touch me; not the guns, not the bombs. That illusion, or rather, that innocence would disappear, in spite of the promise of a brighter future. Eventually, that stable home in an unstable world would yield to an unstable home in a stable world.

Chapter 3

My Father

Abuelita woke up very early in the mornings to prepare breakfast. On school day mornings, I would always find her in the kitchen, not sitting with her cup of coffee, but standing with a mandilla that she wore over her pyjamas. She was in front of the oven, preparing tea and toast for us. I ate my breakfast while watching her. Before leaving by the front door to go to school, she combed my hair, first soaking the brush in water from a sink. The sinks in the hallway between the kitchen and front door were often filled with water because the water was frequently cut off so we hoarded it when we could by filling the sinks and bathtub of the apartment.

I began attending school at the age of three. My older brother and I headed out with my father in his car in the mornings and came back walking with my grandfather, Abuelito. It was about one kilometre in a straight line down Hamra Street from the school to our apartment. We took this route to return home once school was out, walking with Abuelito. As we left class, I would see my grandfather; a slim, well-dressed figure wearing suit and tie, with white hair, his shoes impeccably shined. I was always relieved to see him and headed towards the carriage porch to find him. With my brother, we strolled home with him and, on the way, we encountered the smell of roasted peanuts, new books and erasers from the bookstore, shoe stores, jewellery stores, signs that said 'Sale' on the storefronts of clothing stores, the smell of schawarma and fries, the shoe shines and finally, the florist Abu Taleb in his store at the entrance of our building, will always be among my fondest memories of that daily walk that marked my childhood.

Arriving at home, we waited for the clock to sound the fourteenth hour so we could sit at the table in our dining room for lunch.

Abuelito had a warm heart underneath his rigid exterior. Although he projected the image of a serious gentleman, my grandfather had a generous spirit, protective and benevolent, for my brother and I. He came home every Tuesday to the house with a big bag of candy that he placed in the first drawer of the desk next to his bed.

He often lay down on his bed to read his newspapers. Squatting on the bed behind the newspaper that was stretched between Abuelito's hands, my brother and I would fool around, making the newspaper shake, to distract him and indirectly indicate that we were there. We wanted to play with him! And sometimes, when my stepmother would scold us, we ran as fast as we could along those infinite seeming corridors to jump on his bed. Anchored in the bed, we were in a fortress where no one could reach.

When I was eight, on the first day of class, we needed to introduce ourselves with our first name. Hearing "Rindala," the teacher asked me to say it again and then tried to repeat it after me.

"Are you Lebanese?" she asked me.

"Yes," I replied.

"That's not a common name," she explained.

I had never thought before about whether or not my given name was well-known. Arriving home that evening, after we were all together in the family room, I asked my father where my name came from, and that's when I learned that my name was the title of a book. It was a book written by Said Akl, a Lebanese poet who was among your favourites, Mother. After that day, I became aware that you had given me my name.

Returning home from work, my father gave us each a chocolate Kinder egg with a little toy inside it. Over the years, we amassed a giant collection of these toys. Afterwards, he headed to the balcony that faced the main road where he spent many long moments. That same balcony where my brother and I would play our games of secrets, hiding and silliness, was, for my father, a summit on which he perched to witness the unveiling of reality: concrete structures pockmarked by bullets and bombs, haunted buildings, a mountain of garbage that never ceased growing. Faced with the reality before him, my father's gaze was pensive, preoccupied and very distant. He never spoke much, but over the years, I saw much sadness in him.

I became aware of my father at the age of three or four, the day he returned to the house after a long trip. He entered through the door and came towards me with a wave and, at that moment, I ran towards Abuelita to hide behind her legs. I gripped her so tightly in hopes of not being seen. At the same time, curiosity pushed me to look at him. And all at once, he picked me up in his arms and tossed me towards the ceiling playfully.

I began crying even as Abuelita told me, "But that's your father!" For me, he was a stranger, but after that day, I began to know him as my father, Pati.

In spite of everything that was going on in the country, Pati did not want to leave Lebanon. He wanted to realise the dream of his father, Abuelito, to rebuild the family in their native country. They had been expatriates in Bolivia, although as they began their undergraduate studies, Abuelito made his children go to Lebanon; first my father, the eldest, with my aunt and all the rest until the day that they all found themselves together in Lebanon: Abuelito, Abuelita, my father and my four aunts.

My father completed his degree in Civil Engineering at the American University of Beirut. He worked for several years in various countries of the Middle East as a construction site manager.

During my childhood and adolescence, he was someone I observed and analysed from a distance. Someone I tried to understand because the world in which I found him was detached from the place that had shaped him.

Chapter 4

The Difference between War and Peace

A child who was born and raised in a war does not see the difference between war and peace. That child cannot understand the distinction, it is simply her reality and her world, that she takes pleasure in. It is only once she leaves that she begins to understand that thunderclaps are not explosions.

The halls that surrounded our family room were also the line that we must never cross once the bullets and bombs took over our sleepless nights. As soon as we heard the gunshots and explosions, we gathered in the family room to keep away from the windows that surrounded our apartment.

We all lay on a mattress on the ground; my stepmother on one side, my brothers and I in the middle and my father on the other side. Abuelita sat on the sofa. In the darkness, my father listened on a small radio to the unfolding of events from which we could not distance ourselves. I do not know if we were laying down because it was night and we were supposed to sleep or because it was better to be low to the ground to avoid the bullets that entered through the windows of our room, our grandparents' room and the living room. The sound of broken glass was preceded by bombs bursting and a sharp light that lit up the sky for a few seconds: seconds that seemed endless to me, because those bursts of light that disappeared were followed by another and then another, not letting up for hours.

We remained in our apartment because the Red Cross had set up in the basement of our building and it was now too late to go outside to cross the road, amidst the bombing and gunfire, to shelter in the basement of the building across from ours. I heard the rhythmic pounding of soldiers' boots on the marble staircases as they went up and down at a fast clip, taking to the roof of our building, that became the *mise en scène* for their artillery fire. Those same stairs that my brother galloped down each morning on his way to school, showing off to me by hopping down three or four at a time, now metamorphosed into a vehicle for the soldiers to stage their gunfire siege. A single space can house joyful games or war, quite simply transformed by the actions of the people who occupy it. I understood that these were choices we made with our lives, for the next day, we would be ascending and descending those stairs while playing.

While I did not fully comprehend the danger, I lived it and experienced fear conveyed through the expressions of uncertainty and anxiety in the eyes of my father and Abuelita.

My grandfather refused to leave his bed, and what was even more upsetting was that he wanted to have the light on in his room, despite the warnings broadcast on the radio to turn off the lights in our apartments in order to avoid giving false signals to the armies that surrounded us.

That night in particular stands out among the many we spent in this way. It began earlier that day with thundering sounds that we heard from our classroom. The day was foggy, the sky filled with dark heavy clouds. It was almost twelve thirty in the afternoon and I was seated in class listening to the science teacher lecturing in front of the black board when the thunder began rumbling. Our class window was wide open and I looked outside but saw no streaks of lightning that would normally precede the sound. And then again and again until suddenly the sharp cries of my peers poured out from all over the school. I realised this was not thunder but rather the sound of exploding bombs.

With a nervous look, not quite knowing what to do, the teacher told us to hide under our desks to protect ourselves. Some of my friends began screaming and crying. Fear welled up inside of me, but I managed to remain calm. I did not want to stay underneath my desk, knowing that my grandfather was coming to look for us and the image of him outside, unable to find us, distressed me. The hallways were filled with panicked students, screaming as they tried to leave the school. I had not managed to take a step before I saw, to my relief, my brother winding his way through the other students, his body hunched and head lowered as he ran in the opposite direction from everyone else to come towards me. He took my hand and pulled me towards the exit as the explosions continued.

We descended the stairs rapidly, jumping down two or three steps at a time – but this time it was not a game. Once we reached the courtyard, everything struck me as even more grey than usual, thanks to smoke from the bombs and bullets.

Parents, children and teachers ran in every direction around the court. I held back my tears and regained my calm, thinking about what we should do next instead of concentrating on the sounds and madness that surrounded us.

It was not my grandfather that we encountered, but my grandmother. Without a word, we left the school, walking straight ahead, trying to get home as quickly as possible so we could shelter there. Hamra Street had undergone a complete scene change, deserted, painted over with a grey sky, with the sounds of the storekeepers and the smell of grilled peanuts replaced by smoke. On the way, my grandmother saw a vegetable seller, his cart filled with lettuce, so she stopped to buy some, telling my brother and I to keep going along the road until we reached our house. She said she would catch up with us and I can clearly recall the fear and anguish I felt over not wanting to lose her.

My brother and I stopped about ten paces from my grandmother and decided not to take another step without her. My grandmother haggled over the price as usual, but this time, her hands trembled. She explained to the salesman that she should not be here making purchases while we were still surrounded by danger, but she wanted to be certain that we had enough to eat if the battle went on for several days. As she was searching for money in her purse, a bomb burst not too far from us, shaking my grandmother.

I stared at her.

She said, "Go on, go on, I'm coming."

And my brother said, "NO, we're waiting."

That was when she gave in. She threw the bag of lettuce on the cart and we began running towards the house.

As we ran, trying to escape the bullets whizzing by all around us, the stores we passed were all closed with their rolling gates pulled down to the ground. Apart from the gunfire, it was like a haunted town, silence reigned, and then a few moments later, the silence was interrupted by the sound of a bomb going off. I do not recall the final leg of that journey because I was so overcome with fright. When we reached the ground floor of our building, my grandmother took me by the hand and tried to drag me forward, saying, "Don't look, don't look."

I wanted to know. I wanted to understand everything, and as we went forward, I twisted my head all the way around and saw a giant puddle of brown water. The body of Abu Taleb laid out on the ground. He was dead, killed by a gunshot, and his body was soaked in the blood gushing out of him.

Abu Taleb. We encountered him often on our return home from school each afternoon, sitting in front of his store looking thoughtful, calm, with a little smile on his face. Otherwise, I might see him in his store leaning over, as he smelled his flowers.

The next day, when the sun rose, the world was still clouded by that dust, thicker than the day before, from the bombs and gunfire that had continued through the night. We were like guests in a haunted house, glass from broken windows carpeted the floor, our beds like raised trays filled with bullets, a great silence, and, most surprising of all, our balcony half-missing and buildings full of holes.

Burnt cars and the road completely empty.

The relief we felt over all of this, knowing that we had survived. Smiling, we felt ourselves lucky that we had not fallen victim to all that had happened the night before. With the new day beginning, we went to see someone about replacing the windows, my grandmother went out to buy bread so she could make us something to eat and my brothers and I took up our imaginary games. All was well. A few hours later, the stores began to open and all of the owners came out to sweep up the glass and debris. Life took up its rhythm once more. Soon enough, no one would be able to tell what had happened; except that deep down inside all those who had witnessed it, something must have changed, even if we could not admit it. We were all victims and, with time, the questions to understand why would give way to that daily resilience: taking back the rhythm of daily life as if nothing had happened.

These scenes of instability and insecurity which we called the 'civil war' became common during my childhood; weeks or months of calm and "normal" life followed by weeks or months of war. These moments were sometimes sudden, sometimes we knew ahead of time and could prepare for what was to follow and sometimes we woke up to see the storefronts closed which meant that there was a strike and that the schools would be closed.

As the calm settled after the violent days that had ceased our days and nights, we went out on the balcony that faced the main street. From the living room in which we had taken refuge we walked through our room to reach the balcony. A blanket of shards covered our three beds, beneath which the sheets were still taught and neat. Throughout the night, we could hear everything that was happening around us. But since we were not attained by all these noises, the reality of the danger was ephemeral. It was only by seeing the bullets where we were meant to be that I felt reached by this violence and this danger became real.

Out on the balcony, my father stood in the same place he would every evening after work. This time to look at the burnt cars in front of him. All the cars across the street, including our new car he had bought two days before. I felt his anger, an anger that concealed his sadness and discouragement.

"I suspected that they were going to drop bombs on this spot, and I told myself that it is best to park the car on the other side, away from the gas station. I told myself that if a bomb was to hit the gas station it would have been impossible for the cars not to burn with the explosion of gasoline. On this side, there was a chance ... "I heard my father explain why, to find a logic and to rationalize what was happening.

A single explosion can wipe out years of evolution for a person, a family, a society in a matter of minutes. By watching a child build or create, we can understand the anger he feels when his effort is wiped away by his structure collapsing due to an unevenly set block. We can console this child, explaining to him that he can start again and learn to rebuild something stronger that will not fall. Imagine the feeling of seeing everything in front of us, by us and through us being wiped out by the destruction of a bomb in a few minutes. Without understanding how to restore, recreate what has been eliminated. How to console an adult when the gesture that destroyed what he has created exceeds his capacity and his effort to rebuild it in his life? His confidence can be lost forever.

Abuelita remembers the afternoon when she came to

pick us up from school, during a troubled period of instability. That afternoon we couldn't distinguish the traces of her smile though her pale face but rather the hints of a fragile demeanour through her strength. When we got out of the school, the military stopped us on Hamra Street, not far from the school exit. Abuelita, a little worried, spoke with the military official. I didn't quite understand what was happening. After a few minutes, Abuelita told us that we had to go down into the sewer to walk under the street because if we continued straight on our daily journey we risked being killed.

We followed Abuelita, the military official lifted the man cover and asked Abuelita to follow him. He took me in his arms, my brother was right in front of me. The rest of the way home is a blur to me. I remember the strong smell, the darkness, the circular walls and ceilings, Abuelita's gaze, but how we got out I don't remember very well. Today, Abuelita said to me with a smile, "Do you remember? That day, she was not smiling.

One afternoon when we arrived home from school, we heard the bullets at a distance. Abuelita told us that from now on we are going to put aluminium bowls on our heads every time we heard gunshots, even if they were distant. What would be even better is to sit in the storage room of our apartment with the bowls on your head until the bullets stopped. Those were the most recent morning radio and advisory announcements. How to flee from everything that was happening? Without being able to foresee the end, without any clarity, we persevered through everything that was happening by making it a habit of life rather than an event. And that's how life in the war became our reality, my childhood's reality; the one I remember nostalgically.

Very often in these moments of unforeseen changes, I

did not thoroughly comprehend what was happening. I remember getting out of the taxi at the port, a huge crowd stood in front of us and my stepmother telling us that we had to do everything to get on the anchored boat. The boat was about to leave the harbour to go to Cyprus. Pressed against each other, my brothers and I were walking half a step at a time. In the distance we could hear the bombs exploding intermittently - not knowing when the next explosion would be heard and at what distance. After more than three hours standing, pressed like sardines we were at the entrance of the boat. Rows and rows of people of all ages sitting on the ground waited for the boat to leave the harbour. We barely sat down, and the boat started moving. We were squatting on the ground in the lower windowless level and cradled from side to side by the waves. The movements persisted until I began to feel sick; others around me had their heads buried in their hands, while many were throwing up in bags - no one knew how long the boat trip would last. I no longer remember how we landed in Cyprus, a small island of the Mediterranean Sea not far from Lebanon.

We spent a year in Cyprus, without Abuelita, in an apartment separated from the sea by a main road. At the beach, we spent the afternoons after school playing in the sand and in the waves. We had found a little paradise for a few months while waiting for calm to return to Beirut - while Abuelita and Abuelito continued to battle the reality in Beirut.

Until this day I do not understand how destruction through bombs and bullets equals power. How can someone who destroys become more powerful? Those who aim to silence and increase their place through a wounding force, end up spreading waves of hatred that multiply and ultimately shake those who created them.

For several years after having lived through these moments I relive them in silence. At first because I was surrounded by many who lived through the same thing. Afterwards, it was because once we took a distance through time and space from this reality, it became a fictitious experience not different from the images we saw in films. It was rare to be able to share it with someone who would fully comprehending it.

A blast can last a few seconds, but the undulations created by one blast spreads across borders, time, distance and persists for an eternity.

Chapter 5

A Rose That Will Sing for You, Abuelita

"I have an idea," my brother said to me.

"What is it?" I responded.

"With the money we've saved up, we'll buy a present for Abuelita before we leave for Canada."

I very much liked the idea of giving her a present. Returning from school one afternoon, we entered a store where we bought a dark orange, fragrant rose that sang when you squeezed one of its petals. I will never forget the smile on Abuelita's face the day that we presented her with the singing rose. She was surprised, not knowing how we had managed to come by the gift.

As we prepared to leave that apartment on the third floor in a few weeks, I did not understand just how much I would miss all the moments spent there, despite everything. Abuelita had finished selling all our toys and furniture, aside from those that we would take with us in the boat. One of my last memories was the day on which my brother and I found ourselves alone at home with Abuelito, who was asleep in his bed. In the living room, among the boxes, my brother and I had found some smaller ones. Upon opening them, I saw you for the second time, but this time, in hundreds of photos. You had a broad grin, brown hair, dark eyes and pale skin. You smiled in all the photos. Softness radiated from you, even through your intense gaze, which could be profound and sometimes pensive. Over the years, I had come to understand that you had existed and why you no longer existed here. I stared at these photos with a great desire to know you, all while avoiding my brother's eyes as he sat next to me. Then suddenly, we heard the keys opening the entryway door and quickly, we put the photos back in their boxes. Abuelita had returned to the house after finishing the errands she needed to do.

"There will be snow in the winter! In the summer, we'll go camping! There are beautiful houses with green lawns and parks everywhere," we were told about Canada.

I left with the illusion that all would be so wonderful. In spite of the pain that I felt at times, times when I went to find Abuelita in the kitchen, standing as she washed the dishes just before putting out the lights at the end of the day. I watched her and watched her some more.

This time, I was nine years old, and the journey that awaited us would take a lot longer than a few months. That last day in Lebanon, a day in the month of April, the sun shone, the sky was blue and the air was fresh and cool: a perfect day. In a few hours, we would leave. Our bags were ready, standing in a line next to the door. Abuelita asked my brother and me to go outside to sit on the balcony. She remained standing, looking down at us, and explained that we would soon leave her. She asked us to write to her and describe all our adventures to her. Returning to the salon, we waited for the taxi. Several minutes later, I heard the car horn beeping insistently. My heart beat loud in my ears, a different sound, but no less insistent. I stared up at her, trying so hard to hold back my tears. She was the only thing I could see.

Abuelita never got sick, she never tired and she never cried, except for that day. She opened the door. I looked at her. Her hand held the door open, her head turned towards us, her eyes veiled and her gaze distant in order to hide her sadness. I did not want to leave. I continued to watch her, but her eyes did not meet mine. Approaching the door, I lifted my head to look upon her one more time and suddenly, the tears ran down her cheeks. She said to me, "Go on, get going…"

It was the first time I saw Abuelita cry.

I no longer remember our drive to the airport or our entry into the plane. It was not my first flight, but my second. The first time was when I was six years old and we took a plane to Cypress one summer to escape the war.

We arrived in Canada in April. The sun was not smiling down at us. When we left the airport, an uncle and aunt whom I did not recognise came to pick us up. Sitting in the car with my brother, I stared out the window without uttering a word. The countryside spread out into the distance, the lanes stretched on infinitely and the cars flew by us at high speed. I saw snow along the roadside but it was not the white snow from my dreams. It was small patches of grey. The brown trunks of the trees amidst the web of grey and brown shades that I saw from the window were stripped of their green leaves, standing tall against the grey sky.

We were going to live with my aunt, just until my father found a job and a house. My aunt's house was one of many standing in a row on her street. One after the other, they were arranged along the street in a neat line. They were all three stories tall and built with the same dimensions. The street seemed enormous, with slopes that descended from the road to the houses spaced out at regular intervals. The cars parked on these slopes. Everything seemed so different to me.

"But why do you still have your gum? You haven't started chewing it yet?" my brother asked me.

I did not reply.

"But why? Go on, eat it! We're going to eat them. We shouldn't just hold on to them. She gave them to us so that we could eat them," he told me in a firm tone, a little exasperated.

I think my brother understood that I felt sad about eating the last of the candy that Abuelita gave us few hours before we got in the taxi. I stared at them with tears in my eyes. It was the last thing she had given me. She gave them to us, telling us to chew on them while we were in the airplane to relieve the pain in our ears during the flight. I did not want to eat them, because this time, I did not want her to disappear too. I ended up giving in to what my brother said. I did not want him to find them again. As I chewed, the tears flowed. I did not know if I would see her again, if I would feel her reassuring presence, the confidence that helped calm my anxiety and made my fears disappear. I missed her so much. From time to time, she wrote me letters. I kept them to read in calm, quiet moments on my own so that I could feel her through the traces of ink written on paper that still faintly carried her scent.

The year after we left, the city of Beirut descended into an unceasing series of violent battles. These developments motivated Abuelita to leave Lebanon, although Abuelito did not want to go since he wished to die in the land of his birth.

A year later, Abuelita reunited with us in Canada with Abuelito. She left her whole life behind once again. With only a few suitcases in tow, she made the journey with Abuelito.

But Abuelito no longer recognised me.

Abuelito had begun to lose his memory the year before our departure from Lebanon. On the day we left, he did not understand what was happening and did not remember who we were anymore. My grandmother had him board the plane without understanding that he was leaving Lebanon. She told him that they were going on a small trip. That little trip took him all the way to Canada where he died two years later without understanding where he was.

From that spacious apartment with its marble corridors, two salons, large balconies, sculpted wood furniture, crystal chandeliers, coffee with neighbours in the afternoon, excursions to run errands among the little streets of Beirut, Abuelita found herself in a little room in the house of my aunt. In that room, there were two beds, one for her and one for Abuelito, separated by one meter, with a little armoire and a rectangular window on one end. At sixty years old, she began a new life where she would have to make new friends and learn a new language in a new country.

I had not quite understood that in leaving Lebanon, I would also be leaving behind my childhood and my roots. Moreover, I would be leaving you too, relegating you to nostalgic memory. But there was something else I did not understand yet: that leaving Lebanon was the first step in my journey to finding you.

Chapter 6

From War to Poverty

The frontiers we crossed were not merely symbolic, but real. In crossing them, we entered a different world. The network of streets and lanes were to us like a new kind of map that we had to decipher and learn to navigate, in this new country, through the customs and culture of its inhabitants. It's true that 'there is no difference between you and me' after all, starting from the principle that we are all derived from the same truth. But one first needs to understand how to arrive at the truth that unites us. In the following years, the challenge was to navigate those differences without forgetting who we were, all the while integrating into a world that was different and unknown to us.

Already the illusion of a better life was retreating behind the reality of a country where the opportunities seemed unlimited. The promise of a better life does not solidify in an entirely natural way and continues with the world that we left behind. We had to start over again, and not only by taking one or two steps back, but several, and in a certain sense, we had to start over entirely from the beginning. This was not easy.

Through dint of hard work, an immigrant receives an equal chance, but not quite, because six months, eight months, one year later, my father still could not find work in Montréal as an engineer, in spite of fifteen years of experience working as a manager for major projects in several countries in the Middle East. He committed himself to passing the exams of the order of engineers in Quebec – nine exams total – at the age of forty-four. He succeeded and received the license of civil engineering to work in the province of Quebec. Still, each time he applied as a qualified candidate for employment, his incredible experience working in the Middle East did not get the credit it deserved. And so, he started his own construction business.

When we arrived in Canada, we spent several months living with my aunt in the South Shore of Montreal. After that, my father decided to go live in the West Island to live in a neighbourhood where the best public schools were found; a decision that has continued to have an impact on the success of my brothers and myself to this day.

Those first few years, we lived in a three-room apartment with a little living room, a dining room, a kitchen darkened by the absence of windows, and a corridor that linked the rooms together. I no longer shared a room with my brothers. I was in one room, my two brothers in the second, and my father and stepmother in the third. There was a balcony accessible from the living room. In that balcony, we could see the railroad tracks over which we watched the trains passing regularly during the day and at night.

In that apartment, when I woke up, I no longer heard the voice of Abuelita and we no longer ran down the corridor to hide ourselves in the bed of Abuelito. We no longer had the shelves of toys or the drawer that Abuelito refilled with candy each week.

In this new life, abundance gave way to scarcity, indulgence to restraint, daily unquiet and uncertainty to stability and sometimes monotony, and hope to nostalgia.

My brother and I would wake up very early in the morning and prepare ourselves breakfast. Our lunch consisted of a small juice, an apple, two slices of bread with a slice of cold cut meat between them. Every week, there were ten slices of cold cut, ten juices and ten apples, one for each day of the week.

It was always dark when we left the house very early in the morning to go take the bus to school. We walked for fifteen minutes to reach the bus stop. The wind blew hard as we stood at the edge of the road in the snow waiting for the bus to arrive. The cold penetrated into my boots, a feeling I had never experienced before.

On the first day, as we arrived at the school yard, I got off the bus to find hundreds of students running about all over. It was a giant yard with a large field of green grass and trees on the horizon. I did not know where to go or who to speak with. The clock chimed and the students made their way towards the doors of a one-storey building so they could line up in front of the teachers before heading to class. I recalled my old school building; a three- to four-storey cement building that surrounded a small courtyard, and the small store at the end of the courtyard where we could buy small *manaish*, still hot during recess. I remembered my best friend Nada and my grandfather waiting for us at the end of the yard and our walk home down Hamra Street to return home from school. I held back my tears while heading towards a teacher to ask which class I should join. He asked me if I was a new student and I signalled yes with a nod of my head. He directed me to the gymnasium.

The first day of class, I was seated at my desk among thirty other students while we waited for the teacher. When the door opened, I rose to my feet, but sat down again quickly when I realised that I was the only one standing to greet the teacher.

The clock sounded the hour at recess time, and we all went outside. I stood by the metal fence and ate my snack while watching the other students play games; games that were not yet familiar to me. They frequently spoke of things that I had never heard of.

To return home, the bus dropped us off at the same place where we boarded it in the mornings. We walked alone, my brother and I, along the road, with a parking garage to the left and the highway to the right, a single-storey shopping centre in the distance. We went down under the railroad tracks and came up the other side on our building's street. Upon our return home, we prepared a small piece of toast with butter before starting our homework, waiting for my father and stepmother to return home.

Every night in my bed, before closing my eyes, I repeated the letters of the Arabic alphabet so that I would not forget them.

Sitting in the backseat of my father's car, I spread my feet out to either side because there was a small hole in the floor. I will always remember my father's cars with a bittersweet smile. I now understand that the state of those cars revealed the reality of our life in Montreal, the lack of a stable foundation on which we were constructing our new life. The rug covering the hole served as a band-aid over the wounds my father carried, wounds that he did not have the means to heal. That hole grew bigger with each passing year and my father kept covering it with mats of increasing size, sometimes more than one, layered on top of the other, to hide it. Although this hid it from view, we still felt its presence by the concave dip in the mat, a reminder of the absence of a stable foundation. The line between success and failure was therefore precarious, since we might easily find ourselves on one side or the other as unforeseen events unfolded in the years to come.

Pati worked two or three projects each day and rarely returned home before ten or eleven o'clock at night. In bed, under the warm covers, on those winter days that were so cold outside, I waited to hear his footsteps and the sound of the key unlocking the front door before closing my eyes.

We lived on the island of Montreal and my aunt on the South Shore. On Sundays, we would go visit her. One Sunday, the road we usually took was closed. We took another route that passed by Cité du Havre – a neighbourhood in the borough of Ville-Marie in the city of Montreal – to reach my aunt's house. My father, annoyed by the road closures, gripped the steering wheel and stared straight ahead. My stepmother was seated next to him. I was sitting in the middle between my two brothers. Suddenly, on the left side, I saw a building constructed out of staggered blocks, one on top of the other. It looked like a giant sculpture. I was moved by the sight of this building, but my father kept driving at the same speed. I turned around so I could keep looking at it, yet no one else in the car seemed to have seen what I saw. Enchanted, I asked myself, *What is it?*

My father bent over slightly to look in the rear-view mirror and continued driving. It was a building made of blocks stacked on top of each other with rectangular windows. The blocks formed a labyrinth of pyramid shapes with trees on the roofs. It was magnificent and different from any other buildings I had seen before.

Some years later, my father found a little house on the other side of the railroad tracks, nestled among giant trees, with a very large garden. We moved to that house after my last year of secondary school.

Although my father was not quite happy about it, when I was fourteen years old, I submitted a job request to the supermarket that was located a few minutes walking from our new house. Every week, for four months, I passed by the store on my way home. I waited for the manager to tell him that I would like to work as soon as they had an opening. Until finally, he called one day to offer me a summer job. And that is how I began to work. I continued my work at the register and the fish shop in the evening and on the weekends during the school year for the next six years.

When I was not working, I closed myself in my little room in the new house to do my homework or to paint. The little room was just big enough for a bed and a desk, with two rectangular windows. Inside, one felt as if they were living in a cabin suspended among the trees in a forest, because looking out the window, you saw nothing but leaves. Before closing my eyes, I sat on my bed in the darkness and, gazing out the window, conjured up beautiful images from faraway.

The eleven years that I spent in Canada from the ages of nine to twenty woke me up to the similarities and differences that exist in the world.

I think back to all those moments when I was surrounded by new people that I met for the first time in this new land. I was intrigued, curious to understand them and know them, to learn about the way they lived, and yet I had a strong desire to ask them, "Why?"

Why didn't you ask me, I was right in front of you. I shared your life, your customs, your culture and mine! It was being erased with each step I took. Every day, I grew to resemble you more and more, but only to hide the person who lived inside of me. I had no choice.

My life began in Canada from the moment when I stopped looking behind me to understand the present – when I ceased comparing this country with my country. From the moment when this country became my country as well. The moment when I wanted to bring my dreams to life in a particular place and began to elevate myself above the virtual lines that divide one country from another. From that vantage point, I began to find that my dreams were inside of me and would always be there, no matter where I found myself. That was when I understood that 'there is no difference between you and me'.

I sensed over the years that my father did not come as easily as I did to this realisation which sprinkled my path with hope. He was always comparing the reality that surrounded him with the dream and illusion of the country of his birth, Bolivia, and the life he had lived in Lebanon. As my brothers and I built our dreams, my father lived within the nostalgia of dreams he had already constructed and left behind. For him, he had to start over.

In this new country, maybe the opportunities were not equal, but everything seemed possible.

Chapter 7

'L'Air Du Temps'

"That box belonged to your mother," my father said to me.

He handed me a beige box, rectangular in shape, with metal clasps that you had to push to open it. Inside was a three-centimetre tray beneath which I would find the last traces that you had left before you departed. The depths of that box would unveil the truth about you.

I took out a little jewellery box from beneath the tray. When I opened it, a three-centimetre tall ballerina stood up, turned about two times to the sound of music and then stopped. From the final torque momentum, you had given her, she turned about two times, fifteen years later.

In the little drawer next to the ballerina, I found your earrings, the ones you wore in the photograph in Teita Ramza's living room. I looked at them under the light while imagining you.

I admired that box and all its contents while breathing in the scent it gave off – L'Air du Temps – in a small glass bottle that reflected yellow light, gentle and delicate, with the wings of a dove on its lid.

From time to time, in calm and solitary moments, when I opened it, I discovered a part of you. In time, I gathered together those fragments in order to recreate you and this is how I came to know you.

My father, who offered me passive encouragement, was my guide. With his silent presence, he kept pace with each step I took. He watched me from a distance and only approached when he sensed that I needed support.

And in this way, he provided me with strength to succeed. At the end of secondary school, I won a big prize. When I returned home, my father asked me, "What would you like to do with the money that you received?"

"I want to go back to Lebanon," I told him.

Two months later, I returned to Lebanon for the first time since I had left when I was nine years old. I was now seventeen.

Arriving in Lebanon with Abuelita, I stayed with her at the house of my father's aunt. There, I waited impatiently for the arrival of my uncle, your younger brother.

Eight years had passed since I last saw him. One or two months before our departure from Lebanon, he took my brother and I on a trek through the mountains. For the first time, I saw snow! Through the car window, I gazed upon the white carpet that covered the mountains, with the dark green cedar trees that rose in the background of the countryside.

"We're going skiing this weekend. Soon, you'll be in Canada and you'll do a lot of skiing over there," my uncle said.

We were going to spend two days on the ski slopes, learning how to hold ourselves up and glide down without falling. He taught us how to turn our feet into a V shape and let ourselves go. A fog covered the mountains, but it was not so cold.

The last day was so foggy that we could not ski so he took us to a small slope with some sleds. Dressed in snow pants and thick coats, we spent several hours sliding down the little mountain. When I reached the bottom of the mountain, I could no longer make out my brother or my uncle through the thick mist. I called out their names and heard their voices. I ran while dragging the sled and with each step, their silhouettes became more and more clear against the grey sky overhanging the white snow.

He rang the doorbell. I ran to open it for him and, as soon as I saw him, I hugged him tightly.

We got into the car to go see Teita Ramza. He turned his head to look back at me for a few seconds before turning back around so he could concentrate on the road. A few moments later, he looked at me through the rear-view mirror.

"You look like her," he said to me.

Teita Ramza did not know I had returned to Lebanon and I felt delighted knowing I would be surprising her after all these years. I entered her living room and saw her seated directly in front of me. She was watching television. Calmly, sensing my presence, she turned around to see who had entered the room. She stared at me, mute and confused. I waited for her smile, yet she did not smile. I waited for her to come to me so I could hug her, but she neither spoke nor came near. As I went over to her, her head leaned back slightly so she could keep looking at me.

"It's me, Rindala," I told her.

She did not respond.

My uncle, who was standing behind me, said, "*Bint Najwa* (the daughter of Najwa)."

She let out a sigh and looked at me with tears running down her cheeks.

I planned to stay with Teita Ramza for several weeks. The next morning, I awoke to the sound of car horns and the gentle warmth of a July morning. I heard the voice of Teita Ramza coming from the kitchen. I headed in her direction. She was standing in front of the stove, cooking, and I sat down at the table to eat breakfast. She had made a plate of *dibbis b't tahini*, made from molasses mixed with sesame paste, which I loved so much and had not eaten for many years.

A few minutes later, the doorbell rang. Your sister, Tante Janine, who I had not seen since I was seven or eight years old, entered the kitchen and sat down across from me. She avoided my gaze. I found it strange that she did not express joy at seeing me, but instead acted distant. She turned her head and her eyes filled with tears.

"You look so much like her," she said to me.

I understood that I bore a strong resemblance to you and that my presence, after so many years, brought back memories of you.

"We have the same feet. You are one of us!" Tante Janine said to me, with a smile.

Why did I have to wait seventeen years in order to start learning about you? I asked myself.

One morning, my uncle was waiting for me in front of the house with a bouquet of flowers in his hand.

"Come, we're going to go on a little drive," he told me.

When we arrived at the cemetery, he handed me the bouquet of flowers so I could place them on your tomb. I looked upon the place where you had rested for the past fifteen years without feeling any emotion. Upon our return to the house, my aunt, who was lounging on the sofa with a cup of coffee, gestured for me to come sit next to her.

"How was it? How did you feel?" she asked me.

I shrugged my shoulders and did not reply. She asked me again and this time I could not hold back my tears.

Looking out on the valley that spread out beyond her house, she said, "That's life. You have to grow up."

Mother, she was right, but what I could not explain to her was that it was not your absence alone that made me sad. It was also the knowledge that I would soon have to leave Lebanon for the second time, and I sensed that I would not come back the next year, nor the year after, or maybe ever again.

It was not only that I did not know you but that I could not come to understand you through those who had known you. That I could not visit your village, your house, the roads where you had walked. Not only would we never go shopping in the stores you had known, nor take walks together on paths you had travelled, but I could not even do these things on my own, knowing that you had been there before me.

I could not explain to her that she had been the first

one to speak of you to me, to tell me about who you were. She was the first who had looked at me as if I were you, who had loved me without knowing me simply because she had understood who I was without needing me to tell her.

She, your sister, I had to leave her as well, against my will, because that is how things were with the war. In spite of my desire, both innocent and natural, to be near you and my country, to my family – to come closer to you.

During the month I spent with your sister, she searched endlessly, trying to find the book *Rindala* by Said Akl. She tried everywhere, she entered every bookstore, without success. The book was out of print.

Returning from school, I continued to study hard, determined to be accepted into an architecture school.

One day, I was seated at my desk, the one my father had built for me out of white shelves. The third shelf unfolded to create a surface on which I spent hours and hours doing my homework. I heard my step-mother's voice.

"Rindalita, there's an envelope for you."

My heart beat fast. I descended the stairs quickly to take it and went back up to my room. I closed the door. I looked at the white envelope, sitting down on my bed to open it.

I had been accepted to architecture school!

This letter contained the key to the path that would lead me to discover the last pieces of you, those from your final years. I would start to retrace your history, beginning from the end.

My brother and I had moved to a studio apartment a few minutes from the University of McGill. It was a one-room apartment that we shared. My father had built us beds with desks underneath. There was a sofa next to them, a kitchen that opened out into the room and a bathroom.

In my second year of architecture courses, we were given the option to study abroad for six months and I chose to spend a semester of my studies at Bogota in Colombia. Along with two friends, we left for Colombia to study architecture at the University of Los Andes. We were going to live in the house of the aunt and uncle of one of my friends.

One afternoon, I found myself alone in the apartment. I had finished my work and I went to take a short walk in the area surrounding the house. I walked along. Most of the stores were closed as it was Sunday, but right in front of me there was a small bookstore with an open door. Next to me, along a wall, I read the titles of the books, then stopped when I came to the name Gibran Kahlil. This name was familiar to me, I had heard this name before. Consumed by curiosity about this book titled *The Prophet*, I picked out the book and headed towards the cash register to make my purchase. I sat down on a bench in the sun and began to read it. The introduction spoke of the native village of the author, Bcharre in Lebanon – your village! I found myself captivated, marvelling over the contents, as if I had uncovered a treasure of great wisdom.

Two years after my trip to Lebanon, my grandmother returned, this time with my older brother. Upon their return, Abuelita gave me a pair of shoes, a pair of trousers and a bottle of perfume from Tante Janine. I slid my foot into the shoe. It fit perfectly. The pants were just the right length. I smiled, remembering the day when Tante Janine proclaimed that we had the same feet.

Yet, I did not receive any pictures of her among the many family photographs that Tante Janine sent me. In the photos, I found my cousins, Teita Ramza, the sisters of Teita Ramza, but none of your sister. In the only picture that my brother took of her, she wore sunglasses. Examining that photograph, I felt that she was hiding her gaze, like an injured child who tries to hide their feelings from those they love by avoiding meeting their eyes.

One morning a few months later, I was eating my breakfast in the apartment my brother and I shared when the telephone rang.

"Hello?"

I heard a faraway voice that I did not recognise, a male voice.

"It's Farid."

Farid, the son of Tante Janine, had called to tell us that his mother had passed away.

My brother looked at me and said, "That's life."

The voice of Tante Janine echoed through his words, as if she had come to comfort me once more.

It is true that that's life, yet sadness weighed heavy on my heart. Although I had only known her for a brief period of time during my stay in Lebanon, she had been my link to you.

I understood that she had already known that she was sick. She had hidden it in both her absence and the absence of her gaze from the photos.

The day went on like any other because I was far away from all those who had known her. I spent those moments alone, but I want you to know that I was sad, even if I never spoke about it.

I continued to divide my time between my studies at architecture school and the store where I worked. One Tuesday in October, we had a final presentation on an architecture project in the first semester of the year, which ended in December.

That same weekend, I had to work Saturday and Sunday as the holidays were approaching. I finished work around nine p.m. I went by bus from the store to the university, a trip that took forty-five minutes. On the bus, I took a nap to catch up on sleep so I could go directly to the studio in order to complete my project before Tuesday.

After finishing the presentation, I felt so exhausted. I wanted to return to the apartment, but that same evening, one of the most famous architects, Moshe Safdie, was invited to present a lecture at the school of architecture.

I hurried to reach the lecture hall that was located on the first floor. I was heading toward the stairs at the same time that the elevator door opened. I turned around and went into the elevator. The director of the school of architecture stood next to another gentleman. The door closed behind me as the director said to me in a firm, serious voice,

"Rindala, let me introduce you to Moshe Safdie."

I was seized with joy. I extended my hand, telling him that it was a great pleasure to meet him. Moshe Safdie was the architect who had designed the block building, Habitat

67, the one I had seen from the car as we drove to my aunt's house on that Sunday afternoon. Ever since I started architecture school, I had diligently studied his projects to understand the principles on which they had been conceived. His architectural principles, based in geometry, had greatly inspired many of my own projects.

After the presentation, I was invited to dinner with him and a small group from the architecture school. There were six of us. Seated in front of him, I did not know how to disguise the joy, mixed with serenity, that I felt while speaking with him.

Two months later, I was seated across from him again, this time at his desk in Boston, with my portfolio in hand.

Chapter 8

The Sculptor and the Poet

Tia Samia, my father's sister, picked me up from the bus stop. I was moving to Boston to start work at the architectural firm of Moshe Safdie.

Upon arriving at my aunt's house, she showed me the room where I was going to stay. The room was located right next to the kitchen, with large windows along the walls that faced the street. On entering the room, my aunt told me to take the time I needed to get settled and then we could sit down at the table to eat.

I opened my little suitcase and took out two pairs of pants and three shirts, which I arranged in the closet. Afterwards, I headed for the kitchen where I sat down to await my aunt.

"You already finished settling in?" she asked me.

"Yes, I put my clothes away in the closet," I replied.

That night, after we had eaten, she came into the room with me. As we were talking, she opened the closet.

"Where are they, your clothes?" she asked me.

"Right there on the shelf," I responded.

"That's all you have?" she said, eyeing me.

"Yes, why?" I said.

"But how can you start working at your job with only two pairs of pants and three shirts?" She sighed.

The next day, after my first day at work, my aunt returned home with a bag full of clothes, face creams, hair care products and make-up.

I waited impatiently for Mondays when I could return to work at the architectural firm in the heart of a modest two-floor structure. The building was constructed of red brick on the outside, a short distance from the centre of the city of Boston. On the inside, a world of models, sketches and drawings, of images conceived by Moshe Safdie, spread out over the tables and was displayed all over the walls. The sound of printers printing out drawings filled the two floors that were linked by a stairway in the middle. I felt as if I was enclosed in this incredible world of design, of imagination and creation – a world that seemed at complete odds with the destruction I had known up until then.

The two floors had open floor plans with grand columns of wood. We felt as if we were cocooned by the trees outside, whose height exceeded the building, through the enormous windows that wrapped around the edifice. The architects seated all along those windows worked part-time on their drafting tables and part-time at their computers. They were surrounded by rolls of paper, drawings, models, coloured pencils, for hours, sometimes deep into the night, creating and bringing to life magnificent shapes. A model workshop spread out over the entire area of the basement, with models scattered here and there. In that building, an incredible energy radiated.

One day, I was trying to reconstruct on the computer the design sketches from the numerous white papers scattered across my drafting table.

Moshe Safdie stopped at my desk and sat down.

"Don't waste time trying to understand how these forms are constructed. First imagine, and then draw the shapes that you want to bring to life," he told me.

While he was talking to me, he drew fluid shapes on a huge white piece of paper. I watched the ink flow from his pen to trace wavy shapes, elegant, with a freedom and plasticity that knew no constraints.

It was at that moment that I understood the power of our imagination. To bring something to life, we first need to conceive it in our thoughts – create a design in our minds. Once we imagine it, we can make it a reality.

In Boston, I found myself where you had been, discovering it through the box that belonged to you, the one my father had given to me years before.

One Saturday morning, in the peace and quiet of my apartment, I opened the beige box. I retrieved the black wallet that I found under the tray. I unfolded it and for several minutes, I studied the pictures of my father and a little photo of my older brother that I found inside. In the wallet, I found a little money, your ID card with a picture of you on it, and some calling cards. I took out the calling cards to read them one by one. Upon seeing several addresses in the city of Boston that I recognised, I smiled, intrigued to see that I was now there where you had lived.

Among the cards, I stopped at that of Kahlil Gibran. The name resonated in me, through the stories I had heard in Lebanon and the book by Gibran Kahlil that I had discovered in Colombia. The card was plain, it had his name, Kahlil Gibran, his title as a sculptor, his address and his telephone number.

Looking at the name Kahlil Gibran, I saw Teita Ramza again, talking to me about the statue that was in our living room in Lebanon. I wondered if he was still alive and if he still lived at that address. I thought he had probably passed away; otherwise, my father would have encouraged me to find him and make his acquaintance.

One Saturday, I walked from my apartment to find the address indicated on the card of Kahlil Gibran, curious to know if he still resided there. I climbed the stairs, hesitating a little. As I looked through the window to see if the place was inhabited and Kahlil Gibran still lived there, I saw the woman's bust again, twenty years later. I caught sight of her through the window – the extended neckline, the eyes directed upward and the long ponytail. She continued to emanate hope from her deep, pensive gaze.

After we had left Lebanon, I had not seen the statue of that lady again – the statue of you. In looking at your bust through the window, I understood that I was now standing where you had once stood.

"Is it possible he's still alive?" I asked myself.

I rang the doorbell but no one came to open it. I waited a little before leaving. I descended the stairs to return to my apartment on foot. I told myself surely he was no longer alive and that must be why my father never told me that he lived in Boston.

A few days later, I headed again in the direction of Kahlil Gibran's house. Arriving on the perpendicular street, I looked straight at his house at the end of the street lined with green trees along the sidewalks and houses built of red brick. This time, I made out the shape of an elderly gentleman with white hair seated on the steps of the house at the end of the street. I approached him one step at a time, without lowering my eyes so that I would not lose sight of him. When I finally stood a few steps from the stairs where the man was seated, I asked him, "Are you Kahlil Gibran?"

He replied that it was him and at that moment I told him, "I am the daughter of Najwa."

With tears in his eyes, he headed immediately for the door of his house. His wife, Jean, came to the door and stared at me, not knowing what to say, as Kahlil went down to the basement and came back up with a yellow envelope. He opened it and showed me pictures of you, the ones he took of you so that he could sculpt the bust.

Twenty years later, he still had them.

"I met your mother for the first time at the hospital. It was the hospital where she was being treated. Father Lahoude would visit regularly to speak with her. One day, your mother told him how much she loved the prophet, Gibran Kahlil, and that she was from the same village of Bcharré. To brighten her day, Father Lahoude told her that the cousin of Gibran Khalil, a sculptor, lived here, in Boston. From that day forward, she wanted so much to make my acquaintance. I went to see her at the hospital and asked if I could make a sculpture of her. She accepted. And that's how she began coming to my atelier regularly so that I could work on her sculpture."

I went down the stairs with Kahlil, to the basement of his house where his workshop was located, a small room with a large table in the middle, surrounded by cabinets and drawers filled with tools, paint, brushes, pencils, papers and various materials. Sculptures, drawings and paintings were set up everywhere, on top of cabinets, behind doors and affixed all over the walls of the house.

"The largest sculptures are created in the tiniest ateliers," he said, while smiling at me.

As he opened the drawers one by one to show me what was inside, he told me how Teita Ramza had come from Lebanon to visit you and frequently accompanied you to see him.

"There are no drawers or cabinets that she did not open," he told me while laughing.

Two years later, Kahlil Gibran passed away.

The absence of something or of someone is unveiled in the moment that we recognise what we lost.

And this was how I understood what your absence meant with the birth of my children: the places that I frequented, in Boston, were the same as the ones you had visited with my brother, when he was their age.

Chapter 9

Reconstructing the Past in a Future That Will Remember It

Several years later, I undertook a journey through time in order to approach the truth.

My flight arrived in the city of Cotonou in Benin at eleven o'clock at night. For two years, I would live in Cotonou to begin a career working as an architect on new embassy buildings.

Up until then, my career had raised me above the destruction to a place where I could imagine and create. By going to Cotonou, that career would bring me towards the construction of structures symbolic of peace.

At the same time, this small West African country would bring me closer to my native country and history, which I came to know through the hundreds of Lebanese living in Benin.

On New Year's Eve, I found myself in a room in the basement of a church, among hundreds of Lebanese people.

I knew you, even though we had never met. I recognised you by the looks you gave, the nostalgia that emanated from you, the hope and despair mixed with the determination to never give up.

You were rich, you were poor, you were strong and

proud. In this faraway country, you had begun a new life and built a church with stones shipped over from Lebanon. This church rose like a small fortress in the village of Akpakpa, forty minutes from the centre of Cotonou.

I wanted so much to stand before you and tell you how proud I was to be Lebanese once I found you.

The Lebanese expatriates in Benin and other parts of the world came together in a future that would forget neither them nor their history. It was amazing seeing them take back up again, rebuild, reconstruct, each time, bomb after bomb. They never gave up.

Once a month, we travelled down 'Route des Pêches', a sandy stretch along the Atlantic Ocean, bordered by great big palm trees and straw huts. The sun's rays lay like a soft golden blanket over the sea's waves that accompanied us on our two-hour route from Cotonou to Togo. We stopped at a tiny slice of paradise hidden among the rustic dwellings built on the edge of the sea. From the first step entering into the Casa Del Papa, the sea received us, the sound of the waves enveloping us from the moment of our arrival until our departure.

One night, I was seated with my father in the restaurant of Casa Del Papa, bordering the sea.

"I have a question for you."

"Yes?" my father answered.

"I have an image that often comes back to me. I don't know if it was a dream or reality."

"What's the image?"

"It's the image of a woman. She's seated on a bed in a green room with two beds in it separated by a small table between them. Her eyes were swollen and she could not see very well. Through her smile, you could see her suffering, in a light and gentle way. A nurse came in and placed a tray of food on her bed. I approached the plate to take a piece of cheese when I heard Abuelita, who was standing next to you and my brother, say, 'That's for your mother!' Did that really happen?"

My father looked at me and said softly, "It's incredible the kind of impression these moments can leave us with."

The lady on the bed was you, my mother.

My father told me how on Christmas Eve the doctor who took care of you after my birth called him to come speak in his medical office. On that day, the doctor informed my father that according to the blood work analysis, you only had a few days or a few weeks to live. Arriving home, he called my uncle who was finishing his studies to become a doctor in Boston. My uncle told him that if you had a chance to survive, it would be in the United States. That's how you left for Boston and before leaving us, entrusted me to Abuelita, telling her that you did not have long to live and that she would be taking care of me from now on. I was almost three months old. From that day on, Abuelita told me how you avoided taking me with you so that I would not grow too close to you.

One day, I asked my grandmother, "What's cancer?" A word I had heard often.

"It's an illness."

You left this world when you were twenty-three years old, because you had developed cancer by the time, I was three months old.

During my final trip to Lebanon, your brother told me that just before you died, you could no longer see. Your eyes were swollen and you could not open them. He told me how your greatest wish had been to open your eyes so you could look at us one last time.

Mother, what you do not know, although you could no longer see me on that last day, I got a good look at you. It's the first and last memory I have of you. That image of you is the only one that I will keep with me for all time.

The piece of cheese: I ate it, but now I understand that it would not have altered our fates.

Chapter 10

The Truth – I Do Not Believe in Coincidences

Life is a circle that completes itself with a thread of truth that links the past and present.

Thirty years later, while preparing maamoul, I tie together the past and the present and memories with reality, as I warmly remember those moments that seem so far away.

Abuelita still has that singing rose on her dresser, among her jewellery and perfumes. At ninety-three years old, Abuelita lives in a building on the southern bank of Montreal in the neighbourhood of Brossard. Her life is abundant with the family that surrounds her, although each time I visit her, it occurs to me that she must find herself alone for several hours each day.

Seated next to her with a cup of coffee, she tells me about her life, her childhood, her father and mother, the adventures of her life. At the end, she says, *"Rindalita, cada uno tiene su historia en este mundo"* – "Each one of us has our own story in this world."

I learned that the fat man who sat on the balcony facing our apartment was the main seat guard of Arafat, while reading the book *From Beirut to Jerusalem* by Thomas Friedman. I asked my grandmother if that was true and she said yes.

I learned that the same actions that hurt us also make us stronger, though sometimes it only happens years later.

Thirty years later, thanks to life's circumstances, I was seated at a self-defense course. After completing the five-day course, I understood that I would no longer be the victim of acts of violence that I had survived until I was nine years old.

I learned that we need to run, hide and fight if necessary. That we need to confront that which attacks us.

I learned that we must first remain calm when facing a challenge, orient ourselves, make a decision and then act.

I also found out that all of the metal bits that I found on my bed the morning after a battle, while we were laid out on floor mats in the family room of our apartment in Beirut, were the shrapnel from exploded bombs.

I learned to recognise the sound of different firearms, how many shots were fired at one time, at what distance and towards what direction I should run to escape the bullets. If I had to go back to that time and place where my brother and I waited for Abuelita to buy lettuce, trembling and not knowing what to do at the sound of bombs and gunfire around us, this time, I would listen attentively to the sound of the firearms to know which direction I should run. I would know to shelter behind cement structures to protect myself and not behind cars, because the bullets can easily puncture them and come out the other side.

I learned how to treat a bullet wound so that I could possibly save someone's life. If I could go back in time, I would go towards the body of Abu Taleb to remove the bullets he had taken, and maybe I would see him again, smelling the flowers he sold with a smile and his *tarbouche* on his head.

If I could go back, I would no longer be a victim, and ever since then, I have no longer been a victim. I recognise the look in the eyes of those who have survived and started over. They radiate defiance. This defiance stems from the capacity to adapt through risk and adversity. I understood that we were not the only ones to cross frontiers and to begin anew.

I understood that we could lose nothing in this life, in spite of the choices that we must make. We recover that which belongs to us, even through the choices we make.

Chapter 11

A Home in a Time of War

At times, it strikes me as ironic that my most cherished memories should be those of my childhood in Lebanon, during the civil war that began in 1975, a few years before I was born. This war of ideologies was translated into bombs and bullets, into murders and injuries. Yet my memories are interspersed in the pauses between those times. I have always tried to find them, everywhere I go, and there are moments when I still search for them. I searched for you everywhere, Mother, and there are moments where I still search for you. On my path, I have found bits and pieces to reconstruct you, I retraced your life, the places you had been, even though I had been separated from our home against my will.

We can build a house anywhere, we can rebuild a life anywhere, but a home cannot be rebuilt. It exists there, in the place we came from, that place where our mothers, our fathers, our grandparents, our ancestors, that place where our history originates from. A home is the source of our truth. That source of truth, through which we came into the world, lights up the path for us to follow and our life goals. Once we have been separated from that source, against our will, we search for it everywhere.

"You knew it, even before you were born," a friend

once told me. Those words that I carry in my thoughts remind me that we are tied to our origins, unconsciously and eternally.

Through the travels I took where I found you, I also understood the distant look, the lost expression, the veiled eyes of my father in the faces of those who had to leave without wanting to, of those who had left a part of themselves behind without knowing if they would ever return. Some had the means to connect their (sense of) home with their new life, but many did not have those means. Those people who have been displaced throughout the world, in their gaze and the depths of their eyes, are always seeking to understand why.

All those who have been involved, near or far, with wars, with violence, were able to do it because they thought that maybe our voices would be silenced by the sound of the bombs. They were able to do it because they did not know us, because they had no awareness of us, and for them, we did not exist. We were invisible in their hearts.

Lying on a table, I was surrounded by doctors who retrieved from my stomach something that resembled a large stone – the shrapnel from an exploded bomb. Seeing it separate from my body, I managed a small smile of relief and I felt myself able to breathe deeply once more. The air when I drew in a breath reached parts of my body that had been deprived of oxygen for a long time. And several hours later, I saw the doctors remove bullets that had lodged themselves all over my torso.

It was a dream, because I had never been hit by

bullets. The dream represented how deeply the war had wounded me, for even those who had not sustained visible injuries had been injured in deeper places. They carry those wounds in the dark parts of their unconscious mind, neither knowing of them nor showing them.

The box you left me, I had exhausted its contents to discover more about you and to know who you were. I found myself in the places you had been and I uncovered people who had known you. In moving once again, I opened that box and rummaged about inside of it, in hopes of discovering something else about you. I had seen it all and I closed it again, wishing so sincerely to continue finding you on my path in the same manner. Before closing it, I retrieved the small jewellery box with the ballerina.

Thirty-eight years later, it was my turn to make the ballerina dance. I found the small screw under the box and turned it several times. I placed the ballerina on her little tile to make her dance again and diffuse 'L'Air du Temps' that had decorated her with its scent within the box, to spread the beating of the peace dove's wings.

Several months later, my father handed me a box that contained hundreds of love letters which you had written to each other through everything.

www.ingramcontent.com/pod-product-compliance
Lightning Source LLC
Chambersburg PA
CBHW030824060726

17590CB00001B/1383